Jim Johnson | *Text For Our Nomadic Future*

I0156437

Jim Johnson

Text For Our Nomadic Future

Red Dragonfly Press

ISBN 978-1-945063-21-3 paper

Library of Congress Control Number: 2018950992

Acknowledgements: Some of the poems have been pub-lished in *Blueline, Barbaric Yawp,* and *Canary*.

Cover image: 'Equisetum,' 2017, by Scott King

Designed and typeset by Scott King
using Warnock Pro (text) & Quadraat Sans (titles)

Published by Red Dragonfly Press
P. O. Box 98
Northfield, MN 55057
www.reddragonflypress.org

Contents

NORTHERN MINNESOTA WEB OF GEMS

About the Author

I

When I began writing, I wanted to write about the wild. I knew I needed to walk across a bog, listen to a tree, or smell the lakeshore on a windy day. I believed my destiny was to get off the trail and give voice to what I found. In 1973 I studied writing with Sigurd Olson at the Somers Canoe Base on Moose Lake near Ely, Minnesota. He had Parkinson's disease then and so the time spent with him was short. But I did appreciate the experience. Sig meant as much to the Ely area as he did to writing, particularly to the writing of the wild. His essays have inspired many other writers and are popular reading, especially during the long winters. For many writers Sig was the canoe that carried them into the wilderness.

After the Sigurd Olson workshop I began writing my poetry of the wild. I struggled to find the words to describe the awe of nature. At that time, I also began thinking about my heritage and the Finnish immigrant experience. In my first book Finns In Minnesota Midwinter I wrote about their experiences living in the wild.

In The First Day Of Spring In Northern Minnesota I wrote not only about the people in Northern Minnesota but also about the plants and animals. In fact, as I was writing that book, I became distressed by our (United States, world, not so much Minnesota) lack of response to global warming. I decided then that I would continue to write about the plants and animals in order to give them a voice.

But why poetry?

Because I could step out onto my deck in my long underwear and read poetry to the animals.

Or because poetry has a history of changing consciousness. Writing/reading poetry is a political act, don't you think? It's radical. And poetry in its long tradition is oral. As sound is the first sense we learn from, sound takes us in. It is the trail into the wilderness as well as into the uncharted mind. We know the two are connected as everything in the cosmos ultimately is.

For me poetry is the way in. Only by journeying into the natural world and experiencing through the senses can we develop an awareness of the land. Each poem is a stone placed over another, a cairn or a sign pointing the direction. Poetry provides the words for that journey.

My next book Yoik was a celebration of the wild—the plants and animals of Northern Minnesota. Among the Saami, the reindeer people, a yoik is sung to calm a reindeer or a baby. It is sung to build community. It is sung to build cooperation. To travel to the other world. Locate lost objects. Restore health. Express feelings. A yoik is not so much a song as it is the voice. It speaks to the land. Tells us we are all connected.

Yoik was not only a celebration of the wild but a response to the lack of response to climate change, to the destruction of the natural world. Humans are, of course, part of that world. Our influence and actions are significant. The impact is great.

So what can we do?

In Saami/shaman culture illness and destruction were acted on. Usually by the shaman who drummed and/or yoiked into a trance that took him to the Other World, riding a reindeer or a raven. There he acquired the words needed to heal his world. Consider then the state of our world today.

What can we do now but yoik?

II

When I was a part of the musical group "Remembering Finn Hall," my poetry was the chink in between the musical pieces. As the musicians set up the different instruments for the next set, I would read a poem or two or three.

This is what poetry does. It chinks in the cracks, as between the logs of a log house. Better to use poems than old newspaper, don't you think? Poetry infers, intuits, imagines, what-ifs, the possibilities based on the facts we do have, even though the scientific proof may be lagging.

Poetry is imagination. See Wallace Stevens.

Poetry is possibility. See Emily Dickinson.

Poetry is what if? Let me explain.

I believe even the old shaman were poets. They were the ones who lived on the edge between the community and the land. They were the ones who journeyed into that other world. I believe they thought, What if I died and then returned to the living? What would I bring back? What would I learn? What possibility would I find to cure our ills, prevent our destruction? What is needed to fill that gap between what we know and what we need to know? They, of course, as bearers of the cultural history of the tribe knew the past was a boat to the future.

The old shamans, the good ones, were able to convince the people they had journeyed to earth, learned, and come back to the people to give back what was needed to save them. This was accomplished through the power of words.

The shaman then crossed over, crossed over as in a boat, that boat being what we now call a metaphor, the metaphor that takes our feelings, our feelings so difficult to explain, and puts them into words. In that way the old shaman were able to cross over and fill in the gaps of understanding.

Don McKay in Deactivated West tells how Harry H. Hess in his early description of plate tectonics "had to ask readers—other geologists—to concede many suppositions in order to entertain the idea of the sea floor spreading, driven by magma rising continuously from the mantle, accounts for the movement of plates and the surprising youth of the ocean floor." Because the hard science hadn't yet caught up to his theory, he called this "geopoetry." This was how he, and eventually geology, crossed over.

Now scientists say our world is warming to the point where it will soon, as in decades, or even by 2020, burn up and all life will be destroyed. Or is this just ecopoetry?

III

Wilderness is always North. North is, of course, relative. Chicago is North to the blues. In Chicago, North is Wisconsin. In Minneapolis North is beyond Hinckley. Definitely beyond Duluth. In Duluth, North is Ely or Grand Marais. And Canada is always North of anywhere in the United States. In Canada, North is slightly off, perhaps because of the iron in the land. In Canada, North is west, slightly northwest of Toronto. And even Canada must defer to Alaska.

Not too far north of here, here being Isabella, West Isabella, Minnesota, the roads all end in Ely. Beyond, you must travel only by canoe or by foot. There the uninhabited resonates in the call of the loon or in the sighting of a moose. There the soul pulls on layers. Along the trail or across the waters the hiker, the paddler enters the grandness, the enormity that is called wilderness. Should a wolf howl, the fear and, at the same time, the awe of that world hackles the back of the solitary pilgrim who left the end-of-the-roaders behind. Compass pointed North. Telling time by the sun. Aiming for the stars.

Yet wilderness remains in downtown Ely. The sublime can still be found in Duluth. In Toronto. In Minneapolis. And, I am told, the mystery can even be revealed in Chicago. And in the South everyone drives away from on Memorial Day, the Fourth of July, and Labor Day. So wilderness, North if you insist, exists even in the South. South is where the birds and the snowbirders go in winter. Roads end there too, and trails, maybe not waterways, lead on.

Snowbirders tell me the mystery exists. In the deserts. In the canyon lands. In the rocks. While in the winter in place in Isabella, West Isabella, Minnesota, I put another log on the fire. Through the window I watch the chickadees at the feeder open seed after seed the way my own mind considers thought after wild thought. The way, in poetry, the wilderness is a metaphor for wildness. It speaks of the country within, so far within we can only find the words to explain in the wilderness. Wilderness then brings us in, farther and farther in, into the mystery.

Into our senses.

Into our being.

I remember a day so gray a great gray owl perched high in a white pine. All morning the great gray high in the pine watching. Its global eyes swiveling. The red squirrels below scurrying across the snow, picking up seeds dropped by the chickadees. All morning. Until the great gray swooped down, its talons crushed into squirrel's fur and flesh and bone, and then rose up, blood dripping across the snow. The other squirrels continued on, feeding and scurrying, as if they were humans and the great gray perched above was no more of a threat than global warming.

Text For Our Nomadic Future

Forest Road 172

Forest Road 172 takes you
in. Though there are
signs—speed limit 25, trucks
hauling (*ASS* added with black
electrical tape), one lane road
with turn-offs—you must
go. The curves sharp. The tall
white pines lean in. While
the lone raven flying overhead
leads you on
down the gravel road. What
makes you stop makes you stop
at a turnoff. Beside a bog. Though
the picture plants tilt their red
heads and pout. Though
the sundews leave their
leaves liquored up with sunshine.
The sphagnum moss and Labrador tea
draw you in, inviting you
to step, step in
into the cold, cold as Pleistocene,
wet you bet to your knees.

True Shaman

Sees things that are present whether wanted
or not. Benumbs snakes, wasps. Traps fox
with spells. Stops blood from flowing. Makes
swelling disappear. Tosses glowing coals out
of a fire with bare hands. Squeezes snow from
a knife blade. The true shaman has seen the wolf
with tears in its eyes. Dogs no longer bark at
the true shaman who has journeyed all the way
to the dead. Would never sell wind to a merchant,
give the rivers to bankers, frack deep into
the unconscious, or leave no trees behind.
Sure as there are three flat stones in Sedona,
the true shaman does not need a compass,
its blue needle hovering toward the North.

What Would Spring Be

Without Spring Beauty
wood anemone
round-lobed hepatica
white trout lily
blood root
wild ginger, leek
wooly blue violet
skunk cabbage
bellwort and
trillium.

What would spring be
without Spring Beauty.

Under Its Fur

When a man who trapped wolves and skinned
them out, the fur was valuable, once found
under the fur of an animal, a rare animal indeed,
the animal was not wearing a belt with a knife,
a carved wooden cup, and salt bottle, but a three-
piece Armani suit, a silk tie, shirt made in Italy,
belt in Santa Fe, and patent-leather shoes, so
the man himself, the trapper, knew what was
inside the beast was indeed the trapper himself.

Fields

No longer mowed
only weeds—hawkweed
fireweed
lupine, mullein
bird's foot trefoil
brown-eyed susan
ox-eyed daisy
sweet clover, dandelion
yarrow, goldenrod
and aster
so—picked, bundled, I suppose, in
a cut glass vase on the table
given to wife
who said, *You shouldn't have.*

Wasps

Once an old man went to the wood shed and
as he gathered an armload of sauna wood,
spotted a wasps' nest on the eave of the roof.
He mumbled a few words I did not understand.
Although I was young enough not to be paying
full attention, I did notice the wasps immediately
became timid. After the old man brought the
wood to the sauna, he went back and ripped the
nest into small strips the way you might rip
a newspaper into strips for worm bedding or
out of disgust for the affairs of the world or another
Vikings' loss. But the wasps were gone. So now
are newspapers. And all that bad news.

Why

A pulloff
off the gravel road
not far from the blacktop
a pulloff, a tote road
mostly grown over

mostly grown over
pin cherry, chokecherry
popple, a few birch
beaked witch hazel
raspberry
large-leafed aster, bush
honeysuckle, hedge
bindweed, bracken fern

starflower
smooth solomon's seal
and clintonia
maybe the streak-breasted
swooping song of the song
sparrow, on and on
more verses than
"Nickolina"

but why a board
a board nailed to a popple tree
single word *why*
painted on the board.

Knife

Having waited in a damp boot
for months sock unchanged
only a birch bark sheath away
from the sweat of my maker's
ankle he who made me
a revolution from a revolution
cut out of a mower blade
reforged, hammered ground
and sharpened to the edge
the edge of knowing tang
impregnated with piece after
piece of birch bark between
antler slabs riveted down for
the handle not the measured
template form but filed, then
sanded as much to fit his eye
as his hand that hand that
reached reached whether
barroom argument or
sophistry whether women's
lipstick sin or beauty that
hand reached down as
fast as light reflected
in the stars bright as
righteousness
the way only
religion split
factioned, cut off
and left bleeding

the bleeding
that tested
my loyalty
even
me.

Oral Tradition

                              A guy could
carve the handle of the knife exactly as
the handle of the knife he held, carving
the handle of the knife exactly. A guy could.

The Well Driller's Girlfriend

All day the rig was grinding.
The well driller moved the levers, swung the casing, welded
        pieces together, tightened and untightened the shafts,
        and shoveled muck.
A girlfriend waited, smoked cigarettes.

Near midnight. The rig had lights twenty feet high that
        illuminated the birch limbs tangled in cable.
The driller held a shovel to the spot light clamped to a stump.
He wore a hard hat, ear cushions to cushion
        the all day metal-to-metal and rock.
His face black with grease and muck.
His teeth white and hoping for gravel.
His hand reading the description

eighty feet deep.
Then a spectacle moth flew through the spot of light, came to
        rest on the shovel yet unturned, and could not free itself.
The driller, his fingers mucked, picked up the moth
        by its chalky wings and opened—
the wings sticking, pulling (this is how water comes to
        the surface) free at last

fluttering into the night. And
you know how fine the must it leaves on your fingers.

Old Stumps Decay

Old stumps, you know, decay.
Scattered pine cone scales
left by squirrels break down,
you know, grow caribou and
ground moss, carpet lichen and
then pale pixie cups push out
as if trumpets announcing,
you know, to a world you know
that doesn't.

On The Attitude Towards Hardship As A Thing To Be Avoided

Woe to those so ignorant of the evils of curtains, picture
frames, neckties, cream separators, and telephones.

Woe to those so ignorant of the evils of washing machines
General Electric, Hotpoint, Monkey Wards, and Sears.

Of tractors, mowers, rakes, and balers, especially
balers
John Deere, International Harvester, and Ford.

And Mercury, Chevrolet Bel Aire, Stutebaker Lark
Buick Roadmaster, and Nash Rambler too.

The evils of pop—Nesbitt's, Coca-Cola, and Nehi.
Of Old Dutch, Frito Lay, and Red Dot. Of course

beer—Hamm's (even from the land of sky blue waters)
Schmidt, Grain Belt, and Carling's (wink, Mabel) Black Label.

Woe to those ignorant of Vernon Dahlhart, Ernie Tubbs
Hanks Snow and Williams. The Andrews Sisters,

Rosemary Clooney, Patsy Cline, and little Patti Page.
Woe, and wouldn't you just know, to those ignorant of

Old Crow, Hartley's Brandy, Four Roses, Jim Beam, even
those Christian Brothers. Woe to Camel, Lucky Strike,

Chesterfield, and Marlboro. Don't forget Polaris, Ski Doo and Arctic Cat. And woe to those so ignorant of the evils

of Standard Oil, Mobil, Conoco, and Shell. Exxon too.

Old Men In Isabella

Let their hair, beards grow long like hippies.
Wear floppy wide-brimmed hats. Walk
around holding coffee cups proclaiming, *You
could be next,* in their hands not calloused
or cut, as if they didn't bleed anymore, but
scarred yet, though their fingernails dirty
as ever. Too many holes in their too-big
pants, especially at black fly time, though
they don't seem to mind. You should see
them remember Fred Astaire and tap dance
across a wet dock in their Red Wing Irish
Setters with slippery worn-down soles,
a cedar limb for a cane, and tip their floppy
hats. Old codgers with no place to go. Save
everything. Aluminum frame of an old lawn
chair, thinking about webbing it with birch
bark. Forget much. Even the pencil marks
on rivers, lakes on faded maps. And
beginning, just beginning, to love the wolves
hated so long for killing their deer and
the deer not so loved for eating last August's
broccoli. But forgiving the squirrels
for all of their transgressions ever in the
woodshed, even leaving a piece of bread on
a stump occasionally.

Gray Jay

You might think gray jay is blue-collar
as any Ely guy. Likes to hang around
campsites and from a limb high in a
white pine swoop down and grab a crispy
piece of fried potato or beer-battered
walleye right off your metal plate. Or
later swoop down and fish a cigarette
with its beak out of the pack of Lucky
Strikes carelessly left out on the Duluth
Pack. Then watching gray jay high up
on that limb of that white pine looking
down at the matches you left out on a
stump, you think gray jay may need a
light after that nice shore lunch, that
gray jay is just another good old boy
like you living from day to day. Then
you remember gray jay doesn't work
the mines or cut trees. That's politics
for you: gray as a jay.

Tributaries

Spruce roots for binding birch bark
canoes, knife sheaths, snuff boxes, baskets

After peeling spruce roots,
I smell the black
under my fingernails
for four days. On the fifth
thunder rolls
in my knuckles and low
in the distance. The rain falls
on the sixth day.
The rain falls like pine trees
reaching down
with their whorled branches and
long green needles.
The rain falls like spruce trees
reaching down into
their roots. Am I then
rooted to roots
rooted to the land. This land, you might say, I am.

To Watch A Red Fox

To watch a red fox
watch a red fox the way
a red fox watches you.
To watch a red fox
see the agate, not rust, fire
in the eye. Know the fur that
does not move. Know the fur
so stiff, so still. Even the tail
geode tipped. Legs as white,
thin as young popple trees.
Long snout peninsulas into
a wet nose black as any
east wind. Mouth as black,
the horizon across the snow-
covered lower jaw of autumn. Or
the line across the drum. Ears
triangulated soft fur filters
for frog talk, raven speak,
thunder. Eyes fire agate
with black-holed pupils leading you on
as any hope would do.
The whiskers too
connect. You, if you see
whiskers.

The Great Blue Heron's Return To The North

The great blue heron with steady wing
beats, neck drawn in, legs stretched behind,
returns each spring to stand motionless
like a long-necked question mark at
a backwoods bar asking, *Do you have any
chardonnay?* maybe standing midstream
until the woman in the too-tight Chainsaw
Sister t-shirt clutching three bottles of
Leinenkugel's in each hand and slamming
them down onto the bar like an exclamation
to the point, *This is a hard drinking, beer
drinking north woods saloon. We don't serve
any wine whatsoever.* So the great blue
heron, chewing the frog hopper caught
sideways in its yellow mandibles, pauses
and spits it out right there on the saw dust
floor.

Northern White Cedar

Off Prairie Portage near Basswood Lake
a cedar
four feet in diameter
over a thousand feet of
tangled roots (all those dance lessons
lost) and
over a thousand years old (who would want to
live that long). You can bet
not much to say even then when
one Jacques Cartier paddled by
midlife 1600s
and parlayed a nasal
l'arbor de vie. Cedar maybe
waved a frond. Yet Cartier knew
life on the rocks like life on the bog, the scraggly,
the gnarly thousand year future was not
life at the lake, fronds reaching out
to the sun, tapering into the stand-up life. Yet
rot resistant, all the years by lake or bog. Then
used for railroad ties, telephone poles,
shingles, fence posts, canoes too. Carpenters
liked the smell. Red squirrels ripped
open the cones, scattered seeds. Deer
browsed the lower branches, hence
the browse line. Swainson's thrush lined
their own nests with
the fibrous bark. When winds tipped
an elder over, a branch
seeking the sun

became a new trunk. Just as you,
packsacker, too if you
walk the shapeshifting sphagnum,
ground pine, bunchberry carpet
through the sacred cedar woods
and pause
late in the month of May,
may you see the calypso, hidden, orchid.
May you see.

June

The first day after
May and already
the June smell of
chokecherry blossoms
pine pollen and
popple leaves
the size
of a beaver's ear.
Pale ferns
finally turning into
fiddle necks—it's time
it's time to tune up
to June. Don't tell
the mosquitos.

White Pine Saga

Before
there were
angels
there were white pines
tall
standing over all
tall
dark barked white pines
with wood
so white, ring after
ring of wood so white it must have been
endless
endless as New England
endless as the Midwest
especially the Upper Midwest
white pines so
endless
who needed angels?
Two hundred feet
tall
white pines
white pines with trunks so thick
two men holding hands
could not reach around to
hold their other hands
men with crosscut saws
and muscle
men who logged
skidded the logs on snow
and ran them down the rivers

after break up
to the sawyers and builders who
built barns and houses
churches even libraries
left clear cuts brush heaps
fire
and a few
a few who remember the ones
who came before
came for the beaver
a few with bark too thick and furrowed
to burn
too far too rocky too steep
a few left standing
tall
over all
a source of seeds and shade
standing tall
I knew a man
a man who painted a wooden chair
light blue
and nailed it
high up in a white pine then
he painted a sign
Angel Tree
and set it on the seat of that chair
I don't know what was the matter
with that man
or his wife
she took a step ladder
climbed it every solstice
winter and summer

every equinox
spring and fall
and set a hotdish
on that chair
maybe she had her head in the stars
or was
as knot headed as her old man
or that
white pine
or
maybe not.

Saw Whet Owl

So tiny, tuftless. You might think
deep in sleep, all day sleep, sleep
thick as spruce.
                On a limb ragged
brown/white silence of feathers.
Surveillance ears—one set higher, one
lower. And oversized wide eyes.
Sharp short beak. Rag doll on a limb.
All day rag doll on a limb. All day
until the low-lights and the dim-eyed—
mice, voles, tree frogs—ever the slightest
twinge, that moment
when the wild and
the unconscious look into
each other's eyes, then
the short whistling sawblade sharpening
tooth and throat on whetstone
                      sound.

Love Me Like A Bog

Lay me down on laurel, Labrador tea,
    and leatherleaf.

Lay me across sphagnum moss, solomon's seal,
    and rosemary.

Gather bladderwort, swamp pinks,
    and rose pogonias.

Swaddle me in white cedar, black spruce,
    and tamarack.

Whisper sweet infinities of juncos, palm warblers,
    and Lincoln sparrows. And forever

love me like a bog.

Text

The song of the white-throated sparrow
sure enough is
the text for our nomadic future.

Northern Flicker

Nests low rent in decayed trees,
neighborhoods trashed
with wood chips. On-the-ground
feeders
pecking out pine beetles and carpenter ants
with curved surgical clamp flicker bills
and long velcro-tipped tongues.
The black Jack Sparrow mustachioed males,
drum roll please, wink and drum along
          all Real Estate ads and
Males Seeking Females classifieds
on hollow limbs until,
until female cries out
horsehair bow now scraped over high-pitched
nicelharpa strings,
                    then
  flies off—white fashion rump and
                              yellow flash of wings.
What male can resist?

Along Lake Superior

Whether gabbro
granite, amygdaloidal basalt
or rhyolite,
quartz, agate banded red from
rusted iron,
Mary Ellen Mine precambrian fossilized
stromatolite jasper,
taconite, even concrete, and
fairy tears—
broken glass weathered smooth
by waves—
          it's easy to love a wet rock.

American Toad

Contrary to popular opinion, the American
toad does not have an American flag
stitched to its back like Peter Fonda in
Easy Rider. In fact the last American toad
I have seen was green, dark green, Forest
Service green, the same green as my pump,
so green I only happened to notice the
slight bulge on the snout of the pump was
a hunkered down toad. When I picked it
up, I noticed its belly was desert camouflage
as if ready for assignment to aid the oil-
bearing oppressed. I, however, placed the
toad back on the pump. No call-up today.
Instead, I salute the green, the unnoticed
Easy Rider at home on my pump. Peace, man.

Osprey

In the highest dead pine
the immense nest
the immense nest
made of driftwood
beaver sticks, barn
board and hay
so spacious that the grackles
moved right in
like relatives who will
eat the leftovers
the female stiff, surrounded
by are-we-there-yet chicks
in the nest, the immense nest
in the highest dead pine

                    while the male away, white with
                    black aviator mask
                    cruises high, so high
                    wings an approximate squiggle
                    above the shoreline
                    cruises, then
                    drops
                    drops
                    down
                    talons, reverse front toe
                    and spiculated bottom,
                    talons extended into
                    the splash the size, the shock
                    no other news in the world

46

has broken so, and
rises
talon to salmon
humpbacked
blood hooked talon
to head, other talon to
tail, rises
and flies,
flies away with arched wings
bats dream of, spanning six feet

and I'll tell you straight, back
to the nest, female, chicks.

August

The male evening grosbeak
that danced
          bill, tail up
breast-to-breast, wings
dropped, up to female and
sang songs of squeaking
pump handle and grosbeak
love in June
          now watches
full of philosophy, spruce
budworms, and berries
from a balsam fir branch.

Across the expanse of
swamp and understanding
in the quiet farm house
two hands, berry stained
hands on a wooden table
hands folded in prayer
like wings.

Aria Studies

As the story goes, old Italian immigrants
would pour a glass of chianti, put an opera
recording on the Victrola, and turn off the
lights. Whether it was the wine or Puccini
or the darkness, tears would flow down
their faces weathered like arid vinyards.
One night alone I poured a glass of Gabbiano,
turned off the lights, and listened. After
a few sips of the wine, I heard the arias of
the loons, the oldest birds in the world,
played across the lake. Tears definitely
flowed. You could do this experiment your-
self in Isabella, Minnesota. Though in other
locations the results would vary.

The Fish Head

Don't have sculpted heads, those composers
like Sibelius, around here. Do have, nailed to
a tree out back, a fish head. Dried out all summer.
Scales, skin shriveled. Eyes sunken as if now
closed to this dim-eyed world where crayfish
scuttle along the rocks, minnows flash, walleyes
move into the shallow water now the color of
evening. That fish head I tell you is the voice of
trees. Maybe only maple trees. Yet it dreams
of feeder creeks, tributary roots, trunks that
rise into the night and hold the moon in their
arms. Yes sir, that fish head makes you choose
your words carefully. You could be the beginning.
You could be the next rocks-and-water religion.
You could be the we-are-all-connected manifesto.
Listen carefully. The wind in the leaves of the
maple trees, already edged in red.

In October

As I sharpen a pencil stub
with a plane
to write down on a board
the exact dimensions
of feeling so alone,
I look at the sky so gray
feeling so alone it closes its eyes
and snow falls feeling so alone
onto the tongue of the lake and
feeling so alone disappears,
the sky the lake feeling so alone
are the same color,
the sky the lake are always
the same color feeling not quite so alone.

Cutting The Tree

The tree is, of course, patterned the same
as the entire forest.
As we walked kneedeep
in snow
looking at the tops of fir trees,
he said, *There is no perfection except
imperfection.* Yet
we continued looking for a tree without
thin branches, large
gaps between the branches, or branches too long or
too short. Finally
I leaned against the tree that was to be
and shook—the snow falling
off the branches,
onto my coat, and down
my neck. In that snow-flaked light I
bow-sawed through four
frozen inches of fir
until it fell
from the stump. Then, as I held up and examined
the chosen tree,
he said, *Don't forget to leave
one branch to grow back into
the next tree.*
As I cut off the other branches, I told him,
*I once cut two trees from
the same stump.* And he told me,
I once cut three.

Fir In Winter

Needles flat and worried thin
hoard the moisture
against drying winds.
Branches boughed down
under jackets of snow.
Sap thick
huddled up in gulags
within, within the frost.
Needles dropped
gradually, regular deposits
throughout the year
accounts for decay,
nutrients invested in
mulch. Although
branches broken off
in storms, trees
blown down, roots
exposed, openings for
the wind, the sun
to blow, to melt
the snow off branches.
Then shed those jackets
of snow off the branches,
winged branches, branches
rising up, lifting up
hosannahs, hosannahs
of sap thick as rivers,
rivers running into
buds, buds budding

full of first green, fir
smell, and philosophy:
to be a fir in winter
hoard and huddle up
until spring, then give away
and sing.

To Run With The Pack

To run with the pack is not only the thrill of the chase,
    the barring of the teeth, teeth filleting flesh.

To run with the pack is not only the victory, the takedown
    and afterfeast of loin and offal, breaking bone,
    sucking down the marrow.

To run with the pack is to wait. Wait at the end of
    the nomadic chain, alpha male, female, on down.

The pause then to note your pelage slashed to the flesh and
    blood streaked by flailing tines, hip bone bruised or
    broken by kicked up hooves, right front paw pads cut,
    frozen blood and snow clumped between.

To run with the pack is to keep up, muzzle bloody and hair
    smacked.

To run with the pack is to keep up.

Sturgeon

After People of the Sturgeon, *Wisconsin Historical Press*

1

Ancient remnant like rivers
sturgeon, lake sturgeon, rock sturgeon
survived the Ice Age. As the days warmed
sturgeon, lake sturgeon, rock sturgeon
moved up the rivers.

2

Like buffalo to the Souix, Crow, Cheyenne
sturgeon, lake sturgeon, rock sturgeon
to the Menomonie—
                                        speared
sturgeon, lake sturgeon, rock sturgeon
steaked, stacked, smoked on a rack
sturgeon, lake sturgeon, rock sturgeon.

3

Elongated sturgeon snout, four sturgeon
barbels underneath
                                ala Groucho Marx,
no scales but bony sturgeon scutes
the size of shields,
crosscut saw blade sturgeon backbone,
novochord connecting sturgeon head to
sturgeon tail, hammer and sickle
sturgeon tail.

4

Like buffalo driven over a cliff
the Menomonie herded
sturgeon, lake sturgeon, rock sturgeon
in canoes
    into the shallows and. . . .

5

European settlers found them
useless—said sawblade backs and sickle
tails cut through nets
and clipped off the tails of dairy cows
drinking in the river—
      clubbed, plowed
under, burned for fuel, fed to pigs
        until
supply in Caviar, New Jersey, shipping
to Europe
diminished, rumors
echoed from Midwest.

6

Dark olivaceous bodies
sturgeon, lake sturgeon, rock sturgeon
feelers find, snout extends, lips suck up
clams, scuds, dragonfly nymphs, red worms
along the dark olivaceous
      silted bottom.

7

Torpedo shaped bodies often exceeding
six foot length, two hundred pound weight,
more than a century old
sturgeon, lake sturgeon, rock sturgeon
torpedo-sized bodies
                    with Groucho Marx moustache
underneath.

8

In winter
Menomonie cut a hole in the ice
jigged
          a carved wooden decoy tied to a line
up and down
                    back and forth
and waited, blanket or bear skin over head,
waited in darkness, the spear poised.

9

Spears now made with shaft
connected to
weighted head, flying barbs welded
onto tines,
tines submerged in hole,
not to splash when. . . .

10

Decoys once mussel shells, corn cobs, wine
bottles, dead rabbits, copper jello molds, and
women's underwear.

11

In darkness staring into a dark green hole,
                into a dark green hole,
                into a dark green hole all winter.

12

Even though bottom scattered with egg
shells, potato slices, navy beans, sheets of
pulp from the mill, noodles, paper plates,
or women's underwear.

13

Day after day all winter long looking
into dark water,
into the secrets of dark water. And then

14

the days warm, the ice recedes.
Sturgeon, lake sturgeon, rock sturgeon
listen to the drum
and run up the rivers.

Sturgeon, lake sturgeon, rock sturgeon
log jammed
        below the rapids.
Give thanks, leave tobacco.

15

In Wisconsin spring spearing prohibited
since Prohibition.

16

Late in April
males begin cruising shallows,
backs, tails out of water
looking for
        females.
Male tail beating against the female, not
drumming, not the drumming of a ruffed grouse but
popping, male swim bladder popping, males
ejaculating on released female eggs, more males come,
as if to insure the future, to dance
male against female
pointed upstream, against the current,
the male tail beating out the rhythm.

17

Occasionally
sturgeon, lake sturgeon, rock sturgeon
leaping

     sickle tail standing out of water
slicing
    splashing.
A sign: *Boat or cross bridge at your own risk.*

18

Besides caviar,
roe served in the finest hotels in Europe.
Steaks fried, baked. Heads
cooked with milk, potatoes. Swim bladder
once used in isinglass
for clarity. Novochord a child's jump rope.

19

To the Menomonie
sturgeon, lake sturgeon, rock sturgeon
ancient as stands of old growth
white pines,
sturgeon, lake sturgeon, rock sturgeon
running forever
       Wolf River.

Catkins

Catkins of popple at the time of ice out fall
like thoughts
of random caterpillars, grizzly hackled wooly
buggers, dried deer hair encapsuled
wolf scat. Catkins of popple
at the time of ice out fall
like strips of mist off a long lake
the trail you follow into morning
along a creek
with tributaries. Year after year
catkins of popple fall
like spring.

Frozen Lake In April

Late ice turns white, gray, and black
waiting for the red eyes of the loons
to come back.

Ice Out

The white ice darkens
blotched, bruised, even broken.
The now renegade white ice
must tell,
must tell all.
Dark fallen pine branches
cedar fronds, last year's
birch leaves
melt under the sun.
Their shapes
fall through
to water
true water
clear blue water
blue as the sky water
water that does
as water does
                    ripples
with the wind and runs off
along the edge
the edge of white ice
breaking off, never mind
its past, breaking
fingers off
fingers of white ice
fingers that once played
the piano keys, high tremolo
breaking off in the key of A,
ice breaking off, flowing
as only water flows

past the white children along the shore
waving, *see ya,* as only waves
can wave, finally
going, passing by, getting
ahead.
        As if this could be progress,
the old patriarch wind mutters,
then must rest.
Dusk sets up camp and
looks at the map of ice—lakes, channels,
streams, oxbows, islands—all created
today. Now the water calm.
Only the temperature drops
drop by drop
as water pulls on a layer
a skin of ice, as if reminiscing, before
the sunset campfire.
             And then
the and-then as in
and then
in the morning
        the wind gets up
leisurely drinking its coffee
from a World's Greatest Dad cup
and today
      just to say, *ja but,*
blows from the other way.
Fully rested
hard to live with wind blows hard
blows hard and tears down
the ice, old patriarch wind
from high in the high country

throwing down tablets
with commandments chiseled in
not stone but ice
large slabs, large as
any patriarch can heave
heave against the shore
slab after slab, the shore heaped with
slabs of ice like rubble
the rubble the past, the past
now heaped up at the your feet.
And then. Then
the wind lets up. Who knows
why the wind like any graybeard from
the wilderness would need to let up;
who knows why the wind wouldn't.
Now the calm.
Now the calm upon reflection. A few islands of
clear ice float on the water, the ice having
surrendered, already told all
all that is to tell, turning back into
water, renewing all allegiances to
water. No myth. No ice. Nothing but the
water. True water. Blue
water. Blue as the sky
water.

That Night

That night the loons called
back and forth
                    forth and back
across the lake the proclamation
so ancient, so wild, so unconscious
only they could say,
the ice is out. The ice is out. *Ja,*
the ice is out.

Northern Minnesota Web of Gems

A broken branch
a cry first heard in spring on an empty stomach
ancient as loons
and even before
apostrophed as a red squirrel on a stump
ashamed as the bear who went away upon seeing
        the woman who lifted her skirt
as when frogs first croaked

Barred as an owl
black as a flat tire
blacklisted from a mine
black barred as a three toed woodpecker
blue as a belted kingfisher
built as a boat
burled as two bear cubs high up
        in a pine tree

Collided like rune sleds (*aka* snowmobiles)
conglomerated as blood
close as the money hiding place
creel smell and your soul to boot
closed as her eyes
cross legged as sitting before a fire
cross threaded

Dark as the step sister sweeping the dance floor
decorated as with spruce boughs, antlers, skull
                                of a reindeer
delicate as insect parts
dim as walleyed light
dry and resinous as nine pine cones
double bottomed as a lake

Each morning bright as sunrise, sheet ice, or
        spider webs
easy as smoke or falling
                        into a hole
eating its kind
elongated as lint under the unused woodstove
even in midwinter
evening steel sniffing evening

Far out and circumpolar
flat like a raindrop
frightened as a shadow walking in moonlight
flowing as water down from a mountain
                    or coffee into a cup
from the four directions

Gathered together as all of the parts
    even the fur
given mining matters
grimmaced as sure as pointing a finger

Hel with one "l"
hidden like the way back
hissing like the fish
horizontal like the line across the center
howling at a hollow moon
hugged like bears

Imitating a dying person's voice
insect parts inside
inside my swollen ear
in some lakes where the fish especially shy
in the harang of ravens
into a trance
invoked as needed

Just
just as a hand sawing off a limb
just a woman breathing in the closet
just the wind

Kicked back as a wren's tail
                    after it chirps twice
kneeling before three stones
knife hidden in a boot
known as one who killed a bear
        and never let anyone walk behind
known among the three levels
                    kin clan and animal

Lake with no bottom
life to life
like like love
like a chainsaw starting up
living only in otherworldliness
low unwinding howl after howl

Magnetic as sleep
married as to a bear
mesmerizing as any lake or stream
mosquito filled as a dark hole
moonlit clearcut
moose looking place
mother dead with dog
must promise not to talk

Needing only what can pass through
        a brass ring
never this far north, vultures
new world order
no as in no words for
not a man in the corpse
not one to spit on glass and not
        look back
not to be mentioned casually

Of organisms all seeking death
of origins
old as the brother falling down the well
once hard as birch knot
one who must quickly eat a piece of smoked fish
one who turns the eyes
on the drum the map of the dead
out of the mouth of streams

Past on
past on as runes
past on as epic
promised as your sister

Quiet as one who turns the eyes

Rain as the sound of rain falling
       on an oil drum
rather than an old man sobbing
read like a black book
reindeer or raven ridden from the other world
returned as from the dead
rippled as an otter's slide
rivers speaking in tongues

Saved this world by going to the other
snapped like a bra strap
so many fish they had to cut a spruce bough
                    to bring them back
sought after as words
sprinkled as with chewed alder bark
spun to attract prey
starred as the heavens
stomped like the shuttle of a loom
sung as a rune
swooped like a herring gull

Taken as to the top of a hill or
that other place
there where you were told
the sky was perch colored
the soul gets in
thin as a pin cherry
this world too
through the same hole where mosquitos
          get in
tight as a shrink box
toothed like a pike

Very little is known of
virgin birth now illegal

Wandering as the soul
water that supports us
wet as boots walking to the outhouse
where you might see sweet ferns
while waiting for the world to return
who knew the myths best
winked like twinflowers
winter after winter, then glacial hel
wolves that shit black
worshipped like a stone

Xed like sandpiper tracks in the sand

Yet
you as one who concealed
    the nether side of the drum from another's

Zeal.

Menu For A Recovering Planet

Brook trout no longer than 10 inches
       dusted in corn flour, stuffed
with wild mint, fried in butter. Chantrelles
       fried with red peppers. Cattail
shoots sprinkled with balsamic vinegar.
       Goat cheese. And rhubarb wine,
chilled.

About the Author

Jim Johnson, former Duluth Poet Laureate, has a northland focus to his writing, including Finnish culture and the environment. He has published nine books. His previous collections include *Yoik* (Red Dragonfly Press, 2015), *The First Day of Spring in Northern Minnesota* (Red Dragonfly Press, 2012) won a Northeast Minnesota Book Award and was a finalist for a Minnesota Book Award, and *Driving Gravel Roads* (Red Dragonfly Press, 2009), a collection of fifty prose poems.

www.ingramcontent.com/pod-product-compliance
Lightning Source LLC
Chambersburg PA
CBHW031144090426
42738CB00008B/1213